THE VILE FILE

The Vile File

A Dictionary of Disgusting Facts

Dr James Earl Booker B.Bs., I.F.Tw.

Cartoons by Peter Maddocks

HEADLINE

First published in 1994
by HEADLINE BOOK PUBLISHING

10 9 8 7 6 5 4 3 2 1

ISBN 0 7472 4389 1

Printed and bound in Great Britain by
Cox & Wyman Ltd., Reading, Berks.

HEADLINE BOOK PUBLISHING
A division of Hodder Headline PLC
338 Euston Road
London NW1 3BH

Contents

Acknowledgements

The author wishes to thank sincerely all the individuals, companies, corporations and organisations that have assisted directly and indirectly with the production of this book. Without their generosity and trust this publication would not have been possible. I salute you all.

J. E. Booker

Foreword

Five long years of painstaking research have gone into the production of this book, which catalogues the most hideous, rude and offensive facts and figures from all over the world. The author, Dr J. E. Booker, has left no stone unturned in his search for the answers to the questions that we have all pondered, but not known whom to ask.

All the facts and figures listed in this book have been verified to the satisfaction of the author and are correct to the best of his knowledge, although some of the names and places have been changed to protect the innocent, the guilty, the ashamed and the downright corrupt.

The reader is strongly advised to proceed no further if he or she is easily offended as this book pulls no punches and is thus strictly for the strong of stomach and mind.

Professor M. A. Henreid B.Bs., *Director of the International Association for the Correlation of Unusual Facts and Figures*

Author's Note

It is either impossible, dangerous or illegal to attempt to better any of the records documented in this book. Consequently, the author and the publisher accept no responsibility whatsoever for anyone foolish enough to ignore this warning.

The Vile File

ANUS

Largest

The largest anus on record belonged to Jack 'The Human Cannon' Ellis of Columbia, Tennessee, USA. Ellis was able to place a suitably lubricated 'cannonball' measuring 4¾ in in diameter into his rectum so that it was completely obscured from view. He was then able to expel the projectile with such force that on one occasion it was officially recorded to have travelled a distance of 5 ft 9 in. Although the ball was in fact hollow and weighed only 7 lb, achieving this record is still deemed to be quite a feat. Dr Frank Morgan of Atlanta, Georgia, who took a medical interest in the remarkable Mr Ellis, explained that 'Jack was able to relax and then contract his anal muscle groups to a quite extraordinary degree.' Ellis was born in 1934 and died in 1978 of a heart attack that could possibly have been brought on by his strenuous pastime.

George Stuart Davidson of Kansas City claimed to be able to place a football (American) into his rectum. This claim has since, however, been disproved. Mr Davidson was only able to insert a third of the ball and simply concealed the rest with his very large buttocks.

1

Smallest

The smallest anal passage on record is that of Jane Margaret Wesley who was born in 1886 in Birmingham, England, with an anus so small that it would not even accommodate 'the narrowest of knitting needles'. Dr Franklyn George Askwithe, a most skilled surgeon, tried to rectify the matter three weeks after her birth, but his first attempt was unsuccessful. It was to be 16 months before another operation was performed on the strictly dieted child and this time a 'suitable anus was constructed'. Born to a wealthy family, Miss Wesley recovered from five more similar operations performed during her long and otherwise healthy life.

Tightest

The tightest anus on record belonged to Jack 'The Vice' Vincent of Jacksonville, Florida, USA. Mr Vincent had such powerful anal muscles that he could exert a force of over 30 psi – enough to crush a nut kernel.

Smelliest

The smelliest anus ever recorded was that of Charles Edward Doakes of London. In a letter of 1865 it was mentioned that the unfortunate Mr Doakes 'reeked of an ungodly stench that

evidently emanated from his rear end'. The socially unacceptable Mr Doakes was thus forced to move to the country. It is not fully known what caused such an appalling smell, which was so bad that even the very best remedies and toiletries of the time were unable to stem it. Medical records show that Doakes was unusually susceptible to anal and intestinal infections and was also mildly incontinent.

Most Gifted
The most gifted anus doubtless belonged to 'Le Pétomane', a French cabaret artiste who could break wind to music and indeed to some extent play a tune. He could fart at will, being able to suck air into his rectum, and is recorded as having sustained a note for 16 seconds. After a slow start, his career took off and for a long time he was one of the highest paid artistes in Paris. However, old age finally took its toll and 'Le Pétomane' was forced to retire when he lost control of his bowels and became too frequently embarrassed on stage. (See **Flatulence**.)

BESTIALITY

Most Promiscuous

Henri Beau Champs of Orléans, France, is reputed to have sodomised over 3000 different animals – mostly cattle, pigs, sheep and domestic fowl – over a period of six years. The intrepid Monsieur Beau Champs apparently spends most of his time scouring the fields of Europe for suitable partners and has been arrested 36 times for gross public indecency in seven countries. He is on record as saying 'I prefer cows, they are easier to catch and make less noise than sheep and chickens', and 'I generally do it at night when there is less chance of being seen and caught'.

Most Adventurous

The most adventurous act of bestiality is almost certainly that of Paulo 'Chico' Lopez of Valencia, Spain, who successfully managed to have sexual intercourse with a bull in the city's main fighting ring. After several unsuccessful attempts and some nasty kicks, the bold matador was able to cling to the rear of the angry bovine and perform an unnatural act before a crowd of 20,000 people.

Bestiality Classification Chart

Compiled by Captain John Ross Jones R.A.V.C.
(Retired)

Animal	Popularity	Availability	Compatibility
Sheep	10	10	10
Pig	10	9	10
Cow	8	10	8
Chicken	9	10	7
Goat	9	8	8
Bull	2*	4	8
Horse	9*	10	9
Donkey	9*	10	9
Koi Carp	3*	10	5
Turkey	8	10	5
Dog	9*	10	8
Monkey	6*	2	5
Tiger	1*	1	7
Elephant	2	2	4
Dolphin	4*	2	4
Seal	4*	2	4
Pheasant	6	10	6
Ostrich	4	2	8
Porcupine	1	1	1
Camel	7	6	6
Eel	3*	3	10

*Animals of particular interest to women.
Marks are given out of 10, 10 being the highest score.

Human Comparison	Special Requirements	Health Hazards
10	Wellington boots	foot-and-mouth disease
10	harness	biting
8	soapy water	kicking
6	seeds	pecking
8	onion	biting
8	guts	goring
9	apple	kicking
9	carrot	kicking
4	water	none
4	lubricant	pecking
7	lubricant	biting
6	lubricant	biting
7	dope dart	clawing
4	ladder	crushing
4	aqualung	drowning
3	aqualung	drowning
6	seeds	pecking
8	ladder	pecking
1	great care	spiking
6	ladder	spitting
10	water	none

Favourite Animal

The animal most often sodomised – perhaps
because it is the easiest to catch – is the chicken,
closely followed by the pig, the sheep and the
goat. The most popular animals are the sheep
and the pig.

BILE AND PHLEGM

Most Disgusting

The most disgusting deposit of bile and phlegm
ever recorded was coughed up by Phillip Michael
Evans of Oldham, England. It was so vile looking
and smelling that experienced hospital nurses
and orderlies were unable to clear it away from
his chest. It had a consistency similar to that of
'separated yoghurt' and was 'mostly bright
yellow with some parts being black and streaky
red'.

Most Yielded

On 18 August 1965 Angus Bevin of Glasgow,
Scotland, coughed up nearly three pints of
phlegm over a period of 24 hours. He was
suffering from a severe case of emphysema at
the time.

BISEXUALITY

Most Promiscuous Bisexual

The most promiscuous bisexual was Sall Cornell of San Francisco, California, USA. Mr Cornell could verify with photographs that he had indulged in sexual intercourse with 3456 men and 2489 women over a period of 17 years (1972 to 1989). Mr Cornell died in 1990 from HIV related pneumonia.

Greta Fitzpatrick of Dublin, Ireland, admitted in her published diaries of 1922 to having thousands of lovers both male and female. There is little collaborative evidence to substantiate this claim other than numerous letters and scandalous diary recordings that describe Miss Fitzpatrick's sexual preferences.

BOILS

Largest

The largest boil on medical record belonged to Rodney Howells of Bristol, England. It was measured as being over 3½ in in diameter and stood proud of the skin by just over an inch. It was lanced by Dr Arthur D. Reynolds on 6 June 1924 and yielded almost a pint of 'pungent pus'.

Most Numerous

Reece Williams of Newport, Gwent, was admitted to hospital in 1967 suffering from 'a terrible infection of boils'. His medical record stated that 'He was literally covered from head to toe'. Fearing he was suffering from some dreadful new disease, doctors compiled many detailed documents and photographs, which still exist. The total number of boils on his body was calculated as being 12,568; not an inch of skin was spared. The cause, it later emerged , was a 'bad reaction' to a solvent spray that had managed to seep into his overalls. Mr Williams made a full recovery.

Most Unfortunate

There are hundreds of documented cases of large boils on penises, vaginas, eyelids and lips (but not on all four at once).

BOOKS

Most Obscene

The most obscene book ever published is probably *120 Days of Sodom* by Comte Donatien Alphonse François de Sade. It is a vivid and highly detailed description of a long orgy of sodomy, sex and suffering among French aristocrats and their unfortunate 'guests'. It was written in 1784 when the author was imprisoned in a mental institution, and has been reprinted several times since his death. (See **Sado-masochism**.)

Most Offensive
The book causing offence to the largest number of people is probably *The Satanic Verses* by Salman Rushdie. With its supposedly blasphemous description of the Prophet Mohammed's descent to earth, the book has so outraged the Islamic peoples of the world that the author has been forced into hiding under the threat of death. The reward offered to the successful assassin currently stands at over £1 million.

BREASTS

Largest
The largest breasts, or female mammary glands, on record belonged to Grace Elizabeth Kinney of Denver, Colorado, USA, whose bust measurement was a staggering 159 in. Her right breast was noticeably much larger than her left, but it was not apparently possible to measure

Breast Classification Chart

Compiled by Dr Andreah Coleman, Senior
Consultant Cosmetic Breast Surgery, The Weyer
Clinic, Los Angeles, USA

Type	Size (in)	Shape	Nipple Suitable
Flat	n/a	none	puppy nose
Bee Sting	1–2	bump	puppy nose
Egg	3–4	egg	puppy nose
F&F	5–6	curve	button/grape
Pointer	4–8	point	button/puppy
Sagger	5–10	pear	button
Jugs	8–12	balloon	cork/grape
Silicone	6–18	ball	cork/grape
Balloons	12+	balloon	cork/grape
Zeppelins	18+	balloon	cork/grape

Areola Suitable	Yield	Attraction	Sag Factor (%)
small	v.low	v.poor	nil
small	v.low	poor	10
small	low	slight	20
medium	fair	good	30
medium	good	good	40
large	good	fair	70
large	v.good	v.good	80
large	poor	good	30
large	v.good	v.good	80
large	v.good	good	90

each breast separately. Miss Kinney's condition was caused by a hormone imbalance that saw her overall weight balloon from 252 lb (18 st) to 760 lb (54 st).

Smallest

There are numerous well-documented cases of women born without breasts or only partially formed breasts or breasts that simply never develop. The smallest completely formed, fully developed breasts may be attributed to Xiang Ping Yung of China (currently living in Hong Kong) who, although in her thirties, has the appearance of a young girl. Her chest measurement is only 24 in and her breasts are the size and shape of chickens' eggs. They are however in correct anatomical proportion to the rest of her body and her areola and nipples are of normal size and form. She has had 13 children.

Most Oddly Shaped

The most oddly shaped breasts belong to Marion Leigh Denton of Portland, Oregon, USA. Her 46 in bust consists of two entirely different sized and shaped breasts, both of which could be described as being lumpy and misshapen to a great degree. This is entirely due to the fact that five partially formed breasts have developed in and around the two normal breasts that make up the complete bust. Ms Denton, however, has only two nipples and has nursed all of her eight children without difficulty. She is now considering corrective surgery.

Lizbeth Harding of New Orleans, Louisiana, USA, has breasts that have developed upside down (or at least it appears as though this is the case). As a result they hang in a most unusual manner with her nipples pointing down and in towards her body. They are nonetheless perfectly functional.

Most Numerous
Michelle Vernier of Lyons, France, was officially recognised in July 1967 at the age of 16 as having four perfectly formed breasts. Two were subsequently removed in 1969 and a third had to be slightly repositioned.

Most Yielding
Anne Karen Stratford of Manchester, England, was recorded in 1985 to yield an astonishing 31 pints of milk from her 52 in breasts over a period of 48 hours. It is thought that an overactive hormone (prolactin) was responsible for such mass production. The drugs used to stem the flow unfortunately dried up the milk for nearly

seven days and prevented Ms Stratford from nursing her child born 18 hours after their administration.

Most Tattooed
Kaz Redford of New York, USA, has 79 inter-woven designs on her large 54 in breasts. Ink coverage has been calculated at 89 per cent, including the nipples and areola which are also tattooed.

Most Talented
The most talented breasts were those of Carley Anderson of Baltimore, Maryland, USA. Ms Anderson could jiggle and contort her breasts (without moving the rest of her body) to a quite astonishing degree. She could also move each breast separately. Ms Anderson, a keen body builder, attributed her skill to highly developed pectoral muscles.

BUTTOCKS

Heaviest and Largest
The owner of the world's largest and heaviest buttocks is Clifford Arthur Moore of Cleveland, Ohio, USA. His gluteus maximus and associated

body fat have been carefully calculated as weighing 154 lb (11 st). His overall body weight is 740 lb (52 st 12 lb). Although far from being the heaviest man in the world, the aptly named Mr Moore is very much bottom heavy, that is to say the bulk of his great weight is around his thighs, rear and legs. The circumference of his hips is 120 in. A lifelong victim of a hormonal imbalance, Mr Moore's buttocks are so large that they can entirely engulf a bowling ball.

Smallest
Alfredo Jesus de Sanchez of Mexico City was born in 1967 without any buttocks (glutei). This seldom recorded medical defect is thought to be some form of hereditary genetic disorder, as it is believed that the otherwise healthy Mr de Sanchez's great-grandfather was similarly afflicted. To date no attempt at reconstruction has been made.

Most Tattooed
The most tattooed buttocks on record belong to Mike James of Staten Island, New York, USA. The illustrated Mr James has at least 67 intertwined tattoos with an overall coverage of 98.8 per cent of surface skin area.

Michael 'The Shadow' Loggani of San Diego,

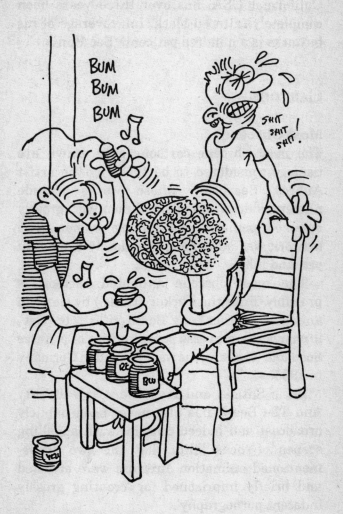

21

California, USA, has over three years been completely tattooed black. Ink coverage of his buttocks is a hundred per cent. (See **Penis**.)

CARTOON

Most Obscene
The most obscene cartoons ever drawn are usually considered to be those by the artist Aubrey Beardsley whose works include numerous drawings of small men with grossly outsized penises, and farting women. The artwork was all done appropriately enough in pen and ink.

The most obscene animated cartoon is probably 'Fritz the Fucker' (trans.) by German animator Gunther Lang. Based on 'Fritz the Cat', it charts the perverse sexual antics of a *Katze Schwarz*. The cartoons were banned in Germany in 1935.

Boris Satiski and Ivan Illanovic's 'Beauty And The Beast' has also never been publicly broadcast and indeed contains such appalling scenes of 'beast'iality that the two above-mentioned animation directors were arrested and briefly imprisoned for 'creating grossly indecent pornography'.

Most Offensive

The most offensive cartoons ever drawn were those of Mario Lutz, a copy cartoonist who in 1984 tried to publish a satirical book of cartoons based on well-established characters. Offerings such as Charles Schulz's Charlie Brown taking Snoopy to the vet to be put down, Goscinny and Uderzo's Asterix being crucified by Romans and Marvel's Superman and Wonderwoman being sodomised by the Incredible Hulk so outraged the proof-readers that almost all copies of the book and the original artwork were seized by the FBI and supposedly destroyed. Lutz avoided criminal proceedings by claiming that he had not in fact had anything to do with the work, which was carried out by numerous bored cartoonists in New York. Copies of the book are still in existence and are estimated to be worth around $50,000 each.

CLITORIS

Largest

The largest clitoris on medical record belonged to Polish-born Irena Litkov of New York, USA. It was the size of 'a large pear'.

Longest
Nicole Bresson of Amsterdam, Holland, has a clitoris that has been officially measured at 5¼ in long and nearly ¼ in wide. Nothing quite like it has ever been mentioned in previous medical records.

COMEDIAN

Filthiest
There are a great number of comedians (as opposed to a number of great comedians) and indeed comediennes who would easily qualify for this title. The most popular and famous comedian in this category is generally considered to be England's Roy 'Chubby' Brown. He maintains that his comedy is really quite harmless and that he never says anything that isn't commonly used off stage. Chubby has a cult following and is said to be 'one of the funniest men in show business'.

Most Offensive
There are so many offensive comedians that it is impossible to single any one out. Racism, sexism and very bad language seem to offend people the most, and most good comedians use a good deal of all three in their acts.

CONCEPTION

Earliest
Mary Patricia Lester of Salt Lake City, Utah, USA, gave birth to a healthy though premature 3 lb 6 oz baby on 7 April 1974 when she was 10 years 6 months and 6 days old. The birth was by Caesarean section. The father of the child is still unknown, but he is thought to have been an angel!

Latest
The oldest mother on record was Ellen May Ellis of Four Crosses, Clwyd, Wales, who gave birth on 15 May 1762, aged 72 years and 167 days. The child was stillborn.

Most Interesting Location
The record for the most interesting location for the conception of a child is probably held by Bill and Natalie Maynarde of Los Angeles, California, USA, who conceived their son Alti at between 30,000 and 10,000 feet during a parachute jump on 19 May 1989. The two shared a single chute and were harnessed in such a way that they could face each other. The event was photographed by Bill's brother Mike Maynarde. Plans for the subsequent birth to be carried out

during a free fall were not carried out.

When Wild West swindler Ewen Phelps was waiting on the gallows to be hanged for murder in Tucson, Arizona, USA, in 1845, he apparently became 'impressively erect' (not an uncommon condition for a man about to be executed). Ellie Rose Morton of that same town was so taken by the dashing villain's display that she rushed up to him and 'lifting her skirts put her self upon him'. Mr Phelps, whose legs and hands were tied and whose head was securely fastened in the noose made no attempt to fight off the admirer (who it is alleged did not know him). The local newspaper in the town verifies that 'a sinful act' (sexual intercourse) took place and that Miss Morton, 'a dancing girl', was arrested for breach of the peace. She later gave birth to a son and on the birth certificate credited Mr Phelps as being the father. He, alas, never saw his son as he was 'duly hanged shortly after the event'.

CONDOMS

Largest
The largest practical condom ever made was for Eli, the Indian circus elephant. Randy Eli was fitted with a giant condom measuring some 3 ft

—ARE YOU SURE HE NEVER FORGETS?

long and nearly 1 ft in diameter as part of a safe-sex promotion video. Despite Eli's impressive performance with his partner Aishi, the video was never released.

Smallest

The smallest practical condom ever made was for a marmoset named Tiz, star of a safe-sex promotion video. Tiz was able to put on the ½ in sheath himself. Made in London in 1991, the video showing Tiz and his partner Martha having sexual intercourse was never released. Director–producer Michael Richie is quoted as saying 'It all seemed like a good idea at the time.'

CONTRACEPTION

Most Popular

The most popular form of contraception is the male condom. The female contraceptive pill is in second place by a long way.

Most Unpopular

The most unpopular form of contraception is male castration followed by female hysterectomy and male vasectomy.

DILDO

Largest
The largest dildo ever made was discovered at an archaeological dig near Rome in 1867. The carved penis with handle measured 18 in and was 4 in in diameter. It is believed to be over 2500 years old.

Smallest
The smallest dildo on record was made in Paris in 1693 by a city jeweller. The ornate piece consisted of a carved ivory penis decorated with a jewel-encrusted golden handle. It measured 3 in long and was 1 in in diameter. It is thought that it was made as a joke and given as a gift to a lady who was 'most virtuous'.

Most Unusual
In 1871 Mary Anne Mottram of Cleveland, Ohio, USA, is alleged to have had her husband's penis removed, stuffed and preserved on the event of his death. It is not clear whether she used the phallus for sexual purposes or merely desired it as a memento of her dear-departed spouse, but in a letter to her sister dated 1873 she states 'I can feel his physical presence within me'!

I KEEP SPAGHETTI IN MINE!

DONKEYS

Most Promiscuous
The most promiscuous donkey ever was probably Casper of Wichita, Oklahoma, USA. His owner Clark Simmons, whilst reviewing the substantial photographic evidence, stated that 'The randy ass fucked anything that moved: cows, steers, Jeeps – even tried to have me on several occasions.' Casper died in 1986 of natural causes having led a 'full and happy life' and having sired 34 offspring.

Most Well Endowed
The longest 'dobbin's donger' on record is 28 in in length and belongs to Sylvester of no fixed abode, Western Australia. Photographs and newspaper cuttings substantiate the claim to some degree, but although there can be no doubting that Sylvester is 'well sprung', reliable measurements have never been taken.

DRINK

Most Horrible
The most horrible fluid to be considered a beverage and that can be drunk safely is Khoona.

It is imbibed by Afghan tribesmen on their wedding night and consists of a large measure of still-warm 'very recently attained' bull semen. It is believed to be a most potent aphrodisiac, though even the most hardened of warriors and gourmets alike have great difficulty in keeping the bovine brew down.

Most Offensive Cocktail
There are literally hundreds of dangerous cocktails that have equally dangerous names. There is, however, a notorious beverage available in a few select bars in New York City, USA, that consists of tomato juice, a double shot of vodka, a spoonful of French mustard and a slash of lime. It is not mixed but served with a tampon (unused) – in place of a cocktail umbrella. The cocktail is known as a 'Cunt Pump' and costs $12. It doesn't taste at all bad.

EARWAX

Most Yielded
Thomas Ian Magann of Truro, England, suffered from severe ear infections from an early age. In March 1987 it was recorded that his ears had excreted over 3½ lb of earwax

over a period of 18 days.

Most Consumed
On 4 May 1981 James Bedlow of Stevenage, England, was officially recorded as eating 12¾ lb of donated earwax. The entire mass was, however, ejected by severe vomiting before Mr Bedlow reached his target of 14 lb.

EJACULATION

Longest Time
The longest official time recorded for continuous ejaculation is 21.6 seconds by Ulrich Larrson of Jonkoping, Sweden. Mr Larrson ejaculated 42 times during the test and on each separate ejaculation excreted seminal fluid.

Shortest Time
The shortest time recorded for ejaculation is 0.4 of a second by Dolph Lindemann of Bergen, Norway, now living in Orebro, Sweden. Mr Lindemann ejaculated (secreted) only once in the 12 tests in which he took part. Single spasm ejaculation is not a condition known to sexual therapists and it is therefore believed that Mr Lindemann was able to do it voluntarily.

Greatest Distance Attained
Horst Willem Shultz of Hamburg, Germany,
was recorded on 19 May 1986 to project a 'substantial' amount of seminal fluid a distance of
18 ft 9 in. His penis measured an erect 7½ in
at the time of ejaculation.

Highest Altitude Attained
The highest altitude gained by ejaculated semen
is 12 ft 4 in by Horst Willem Shultz of Hamburg,
Germany, on 17 May 1986. Herr Shultz is now
paid the equivalent of £3000 per performance
and is in great demand.

Greatest Speed Attained
The greatest 'muzzle' velocity recorded for
ejaculated semen is 42.7 mph by Horst Willem
Shultz of Hamburg, Germany, on 19 May 1986.

Most Frequent
The greatest number of stimulated ejaculations
over a period of 12 hours is 34 by Magnus 'Mags'
Stenmark of Stockholm, Sweden. Mr Stenmark
attained a staggering 544 separate ejaculations
during the test, at the end of which he was said
to be 'a little tired'.

Most Spectacular

Greg Valentine of New York City, USA, is recorded on film as having produced the most spectacular display when he ejaculated 'huge amounts of semen in a great fountain of fornication'. Twelve ejaculations were recorded, each one delivering a large amount of fluid to a height in excess of 24 in.

ERECTION

Fastest

Lars Peter Sorrenson of Stockholm, Sweden, was able to attain a complete erection of his 5¾ in penis in 3.9 seconds. He was able to repeat this feat several times in the space of two hours.

Slowest

Matt 'The Snake' Sellers of Los Angeles, USA, is recorded on video as taking nearly two hours – 118 minutes – to reach a 'suitable' erection with his 5½ in (flaccid), 8¼ in (erect) penis. Exasperated director Berni Cornelious can be heard shouting encouragement then insults at Sellers, who replies 'I'm having a bad day.'

Longest Sustained

James 'Jimmy The Pole' Preston of Baltimore, USA, is one of many sufferers of PEPS (Prolonged Erectile Penis Syndrome). The unfortunate Mr Preston has had a fully erect 5½ in penis for nearly 12 years – 4234 days. Apart from being socially unacceptable, Jimmy has a great deal of difficulty urinating. He has, however, so far resisted the temptation of the numerous surgical solutions to his problem that are available.

FAECES

Longest

The longest human faeces ever verified were produced by Carl Simms of Dallas, Texas, USA, on 16 January 1989. The remarkable Mr Simms managed to extrude a 'staggering turd' over a period of two hours and 12 minutes that was officially measured at 12 ft 2 in. The width of the excretia was 'a remarkably consistent' 1 in for the first 4 ft 3 in, then tapered to between ¾ in and ½ in for the remainder. Mr Simms is barred from 134 washrooms in the state.

Faeces Classification Chart

Compiled by Michael Sutton-Hope, Health &
Hygiene Consultant, H&H Ltd

Type	Size (in)	Shape	Smell	Unusual Content
Peanut	¾	round	2	seeds
Marble	½	round	3	nuts
Cluster	1–4	oval	4	sweetcorn
Spray Jet	–	funnel	9	curry
Niagara Falls	–	waterfall	9	ham
Wet Gravel	–	waterfall	9	curry/ham
Gravytrain	–	tap	9	water
Captain's Log	5+	log	7	sweetcorn
Twister	12+	ribbon	7	hair
Twins	4 × 2	2 × oval	7	nuts
Stuck On U	3–8	pile	8	sweetcorn
Big Bomber	5 × 4	oval	8	blood

Marks are given out of 10, 10 being the highest score.

Stain/Block	Pain & Discomfort		Noise & Splash		Number of Wipes
1	P1	D1	N1	S2	1
1	P1	D2	N2	S3	1
2	P2	D3	N4	S4	3
9	P2	D6	N6	S4	6–25
3	P3	D5	N7	S5	10
3	P4	D6	N7	S6	15
2	P2	D6	N6	S5	15
10	P8	D8	N3	S3	9
9	P7	D8	N3	S2	5
8	P6	D7	N7	S7	8
9	P6	D9	N2	S2	30
10	P10	D10	N9	S9	2

Widest

The widest specimen on medical record was passed by Peter James 'The Stool' Gifford of Bradford, England. The 21 st office caretaker managed to produce faeces measuring 4½ in in diameter for the majority of its 8½ in length. Mr Gifford, who suffers from severe anal fissures, says he has 'done bigger ones', but there is no evidence to substantiate this claim. The record-breaking stool has since been preserved in alcohol.

On 5 August 1983 in a certain public house near Manchester, England, a human stool measuring 8¼ in in diameter and 32 in in length was found in one of the toilet cubicles. It was almost certainly constructed and placed there as a practical joke, but as yet no one has admitted to being involved, nor are there any reliable witnesses.

Thinnest

The thinnest faeces ever verified by medical records were produced by Mary Jane Ford of Chicago, Illinois, USA. Over a period of seven days Ms Ford passed six stools, none of which were more than ¼ in wide, the longest being 7¾ in in length.

Most Numerous
In 1987 William Wilke of Manchester, England, was officially recorded as having provided a single specimen that consisted of 84 separate parts.

Most Constipated
The most constipated person on medical record was Henry Morton Wilfred Williamson of London. His medical record of 1905 states that he went for a period of 8 months 16 days without moving his bowels. The unfortunate Mr Williamson died as a result of his self-imposed ordeal from a strangulated hernia and ruptured intestine. He suffered from extremely painful anal fissures that prompted him to alter his diet and refuse to move his bowels. The coroner's report stated that there was over 58 lb of faeces in his badly swollen intestines.

Most Yielding
The most faeces ever yielded over a period of 24 hours is 21½ lb by Frederick Caines of Seattle, Washington, USA. The excessive amount was enema-induced shortly before Mr Caines underwent an operation for a large hernia.

— DID YOU SAY SINK OR STINK?

Most Smelly

In 1924 at a certain public house in London, a portly gentleman was seen to enter the toilets where he remained for some time. After a great deal of 'noise and splashing' he emerged apparently relieved and left (without buying a drink). In the space of just a few minutes a 'terrible smell' filled the crowded pub. It was so awful that the entire building had to be evacuated and was not fit for 'public occupation for over a week after'. The source of the hum was a large amount of human faeces stuck in and around the toilet basin. The perpetrator was never seen in the pub again.

Greatest Distance Attained

The greatest distance attained for an expelled faeces is 3 ft 5 in by Jack 'The Vice' Vincent of Jacksonville, Florida, USA. (See **Anus**.)

The greatest distance for a jet of diarrhoea is 22 ft 5 in, attained by Corey Edwards of Sydney, Australia, on 12 December 1986. He was lying on his stomach at the time and suffering from gastroenteritis.

Greatest Amount Eaten

Marco Giovanni of New York, USA, 'eats shit' for a living. The unusual performer has publicly

eaten 3986 (at the last count) different varieties
of faeces (including human) over a period of
seven years. Mr Giovanni lightly fries his
offerings in vegetable oil and usually eats them
with 'a little salt, pepper, garlic and sometimes
tomato ketchup'. The meal is also generally
accompanied with chips (cow chips of course) and
a glass of red wine. His favourite 'dish' is Bear
Chip Fritters, though he says that 'they can
sometimes be a bit grizzly' . . .

FETISHISM

Most Common
The most common fetish (an inanimate object
which becomes the focus of abnormal sexual
interest) is underwear. Such fetishism manifests
itself in an unhealthy temptation to steal and
hoard the underwear (in most cases the
knickers) of someone (usually female) who is
generally known to the person involved (women
rarely steal men's underwear). Such behaviour
is usually regarded as a perverse misdemeanour.

Most Unusual
The most unusual fetish is, in my opinion, the
eating of a loved one's toenail clippings. Shoe

Fetish Classification Chart

Compiled by Dr Christopher Clark Ph.D., The
Pennmore Institute, New Jersey, USA. Author of
The Root Of All Evil and *Sexual Psychiatry*

Fetish Object	Common or Rare
Panties (clean)	v.common
Panties (soiled)	common
Stockings	common
Brassieres	common
Shoes	common
Gloves	v.common
Plasters	rare
Tampons	rare
Toe/Fingernails	rare
Hair	v.common
Lipstick/Cosmetics	common
Faeces	v.rare
Urine	v.rare
Blood	v.rare
Corpse	v.rare
Jewellery	common
Washcloth/Towel	common
Automobile	common
Bicycle Seat	rare
Handbag	common
Handkerchief	v.common

Marks are given out of 10, 10 being the highest score.

Degree of Perversity	Health Risk	Senses Gratified
2	none	smell/touch
4	high risk	smell/touch
3	little	touch/smell
2	little	touch/smell
4	low risk	touch/smell
2	low risk	touch/smell
6	high risk	smell/taste
8	high risk	smell/taste
8	low risk	sight/taste
2	some risk	touch/smell
5	none	touch/sight
8	high risk	touch/smell
8	high risk	smell/taste
8	high risk	taste
10	high risk	touch/sight
2	none	touch/sight
4	some risk	touch/smell
2	some risk	touch/sight
5	some risk	smell/touch
4	none	smell/sight
2	some risk	smell/touch

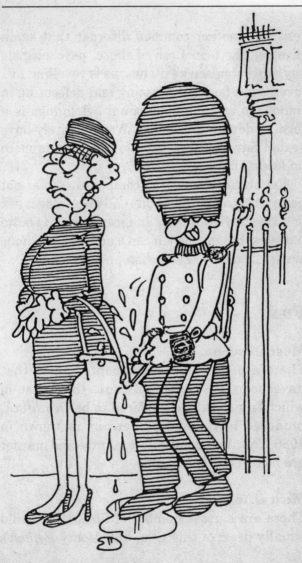

57

fetish is another common disorder that again involves the feet. Both of these, psychologists say, are submissive fetishes, as is revelling in a loved one's faeces. Urinating and defecating in handbags and other personal belongings is a form of dominating fetish. Women rarely have sexual fetishes; they tend to concentrate more on foodstuffs.

'Fetishism is a way of compensating for not being able to get what you really want, be it sex or strawberries or both. In most cases it is quite harmless but in others it can lead to more serious sexual deviancy.' Dr Christopher Clark Ph.D.

FILM

Most Obscene
There are many well-documented films that have been classed as obscene, the worst of which is generally considered to be *Deathfuck*, produced in Holland by persons unknown in 1986. The film's scenes of ritual rape and murder are believed to be genuine.

Most Offensive
There are a great number of films that would equally deserve this title, but *Monty Python's*

Life of Brian (1979) is still quoted by film buffs as causing the most fuss when it was released. It concerns a character (Brian) who is mistaken for the Messiah. Church leaders were understandably upset, as were a great number of God-fearing folk. The film, however, as with most things, gained a great deal from its notoriety and has since been broadcast in its entirety on television around the world.

Most Sexual Acts
Caligula's Last Stand (1986), directed by Dino Bellini of Italy, is set in and around a mass orgy. It boasts a 'sexual act in every frame' and is 2 hours 46 minutes in duration. Seventy-eight extras were used in the film which was aptly described in one movie journal as being 'full of action and adventure'.

Most Violent Acts
The two-hour feature film *Violent Hollywood* (1990) is a compilation of the 'very best' film violence from 1921 to 1989 and contains 7160 separate acts of brutality (nearly one every second).

Most Appearances in Pornographic Films
Caroline 'Lacy' Stokes of Los Angeles, California,

USA, appeared in 3467 catalogued pornographic movies between 1965 and 1979, an average of 231 a year.

'Slim' Jim Harrison has appeared in 2649 pornographic films in a career that began in 1972. Although he still does the odd cameo 'roll' from time to time, I am reliably informed (by his agent) that 51-year-old Mr Harrison is 'not up to much these days'.

FLATULENCE

Loudest Fart
The loudest fart ever officially recorded was performed by David Warren Baker of Rochester, New York, USA. The fart was measured at 84 decibels over a time of 2.6 seconds at a famous recording studio in the city. A spokesman for the studio said 'It is one of our most popular recordings.'

Most Prolonged
Bernard Clemmens of London managed to sustain a fart for an officially recorded time of 2 minutes 42 seconds on 14 December 1991. He claims to have farted for 3 minutes 16 seconds at a dinner dance in Guildford, England, on 8

Fart Classification Chart

Compiled by Professor David Redwood I. Chem. E.,
Specialist Consultant on the Dispersion of
Obnoxious Gases

Type	Noise	Duration (secs)	Smell	Contamination Area (sq ft)
Pip	2	0.25	2	12
Pop	3	0.50	3	16
Whiffy	4	1	6	20
Screamer	9	5	9	50
Thunder	10	8	10	100
S.B.D.	0	5	10	100
Ripper	8	12	10	100
S'Wetty	9	8	10	100
Repeater	8–4	20	10	100
Piss Pip	5	0.75	5	10
Potty Pop	8	0.75	9	50
Motorbike	7	10	9	50

Marks are given out of 10, 10 being the highest score.

Dispersal Time (sec)	Residual Contamination	Evasive Action
5	none	hold breath
10	none	hanky
15	none	fanning
30	slight	run away
60	slight	run/close door
60	slight	none
50	heavy	run/close door
50	v.heavy	run/close door
60	slight	run/close door
30	slight	stay in cubicle
50	heavy	leave restroom
60	slight	run away

January 1989. Alas, all of his reluctant witnesses fled the scene before any time could be verified.

Most Smelly
The smelliest fart ever unleashed was that of Corbin Russel of Sheffield, England, during a large conference in 1974. Some 1374 of the 1500 delegates were noted to be visibly disturbed by the unpleasant whiff (waving agenda sheets, coughing and covering their mouths with handkerchiefs). Proceedings were disrupted for 17 minutes while the air conditioning was switched on to full power. The embarrassed Mr Russel, whose 6.8 second videotape-recorded fart was responsible, left the conference hall and went home, the repercussions of the unfortunate event costing him his job.

Fart Burning
'Sam' Yakkashima of Tokyo, Japan, was video-taped on 18 May 1991 setting alight (popping) 89 farts in one minute. The methane was provided by eight assistants wearing blue flame-proof porous shorts.

Most Talented
'Le Pétomane', the famous French cabaret artiste, was able to produce a fart in notes

Bottom A to Top C. He could fart any tune
requested (without music) and could produce a
staccato of five farts a second, although it is
suggested that he achieved this by simply
clenching his damp buttocks. (See **Anus**.)

FOOD

Most Unpleasant Dish
From sheep's eyeballs to monkey brains and
rams' testicles, the international obsession with
serving revolting food is mind-numbing. Insects,
faeces, even human flesh, everything vile one
could possibly mention is consumed by somebody
every day either by choice or by necessity. To
choose a single dish is beyond my capacity: I can
only say that the worst meal I have ever been
offered was a raw black inky squid in eastern
Spain. Some people love squid, I do not.

Most Offensive Dish
Many religions in the world consider certain
types of meat sacred or unclean and followers of
such religions are deeply offended if they are
offered that meat, even if it is by mistake.

Nutritional Value of Human Products Classification Chart

Compiled by Dr Natalie Quinn, Consultant Nutritionist and Senior Advisor to the US Armed Forces. Author of *The Cannibal Factor* (1985)

Type	Protein	Carbohydrate	Fat
Breast Milk*	good	good	high
Skin*	good	nil	low
Blood*	v.low	v.low	low
Flesh*	good	v.low	high
Faeces	low	low	low
Urine*	low	good	low
Semen*	good	low	low
Nails*	good	nil	low
Vaginal Fluid*	low	low	low
Bile	good	low	low
Earwax*	low	nil	high
Nasal Mucus	good	low	low
Saliva*	poor	poor	poor
Hair	low	nil	nil
Tears*	low	low	nil
Penile Fluid	low	low	nil

*By-products that may in certain circumstances keep a person alive.
All human excreta is potentially hazardous to the health of another human being, and therefore correct preparation is essential wherever possible.

Energy	Vitamins	Others	Health Risk
good	high	calcium	negligible
high	low	salt	negligible
good	low	–	v.high
high	good	–	high
low	low	fibre	v.high
low	low	water	low
good	good	–	high
low	low	calcium	negligible
low	low	water	low
low	low	water	high
good	low	–	negligible
low	low	–	v.high
poor	poor	water	high
poor	poor	–	negligible
poor	poor	salt water	negligible
poor	poor	water	high

Most Obscene Dish

A yak's erect penis complete with scrotum and stuffed with nuts and dried fruit is without doubt the most obscene dish I have ever seen. Imaginative and difficult to prepare properly it may have been, but it did not whet my appetite one iota.

GHOST

Most Offensive

The rudest ghost on record is that of Russian Count Vladimir Bartollski. The Count is often seen roaming the streets of Gorki and surrounding villages with a 'monstrous erection', offending dignitaries and peasants alike. Legend has it that the Count was 'assassinated whilst making love to his mistress'.

Most Sexually Active

There are many reported cases of women and men who claim to have been raped or sexually abused by ghosts and poltergeists. In many cases the abused persons have passed polygraph (lie detector) tests when reliving their experiences. Science has no reliable explanation for these occurrences; psychiatrists, on the other hand,

have numerous theories on the subject.

HALITOSIS

Most Horrible
Keith Waite of Sutton Coldfield, England, had such incredibly bad breath that he lost his job, his wife and his friends. 'It wasn't my fault, I tried everything, nothing worked,' Mr Waite said. 'My doctor told me that almost everyone gets bad breath at some time in their life, and that it would clear up. But mine didn't, it got worse ... it really was horrible.' Mr Waite's halitosis was caused by a strain of bacteria living in his stomach. After an intensive campaign of drugs and potions the problem was finally cured. Mr Waite has since set up The Halitosis Helpline. 'No one should have to go through what I went through and not have a sympathetic shoulder to cry on.' Dr Michael Verge, Waite's GP, says the case was the worst he had treated in 37 years.

Most Unfortunate
My dentist (not any more) suddenly developed chronic halitosis that lasted more than three years. Visiting the dentist is generally an

unpleasant enough experience without the added burden of being forced to inhale horrendously bad breath.

HAND SIGNALS

Most Offensive

The most offensive hand signal available is generally considered to be the making of a fist with the hand while leaving the middle finger extended. This is then waved vertically (with the knuckles facing outwards) at the person or persons whom it is your intention to offend deeply. In extreme cases this action may be accompanied by a restraining grip at the elbow by the other hand. The person using this gesture is suggesting that the extended digit be stuck up the recipient's anus. The gesture has its origins in the Middle Ages where a dominant sodomite would place his longest finger in the rectum of a submissive partner whom he was about to sodomise.

A similar gesture was also much used in ancient times by both the Greeks and the Romans. Placing a finger up the anus of a slave (usually female) was a distinct form of domination. In modern times the gesture is used

purely as one of utter contempt and is often accompanied by the loud verbal statement, 'Fuck you, arsehole.'

Most Often Used
The most often used offensive hand signal is generally regarded to be a ring made from the thumb and forefinger of either hand that is then waved vigorously at the person or persons to be offended (usually male). The gesture implies that said person frequently indulges in masturbation and is as such a wanker. When the same gesture is delivered from the forehead it implies that the recipient is a dickhead, or stupid person.

HERNIA

Largest
James Lee of Palm Beach, Florida, USA, was admitted to hospital on 8 January 1987 with an enormous hernia that measured approximately 11 in in diameter. 'An unusual amount of intestine had broken through the stomach muscles; it is the largest hernia I have ever recorded,' consultant surgeon James Foster stated at the time. After a two-hour operation 68-year-old Mr Lee made a full recovery.

Most Numerous

Wayne Gifford of Bolton, England, was accredited in 1965 as having eight hernias. All of them were corrected with surgery. Dr Alan Phillips explained: 'It is very unusual to have so many.' Mr Gifford said, 'I did a lot of lifting . . . I was pretty stupid I suppose.'

Most Unfortunate

John B. Ward of Atlanta, Georgia, USA, is one of many men whose hernia squeezed its way into his scrotum, which in this case swelled to the size of a grapefruit. This is a very painful experience and rapid surgery is required if long-term damage is to be avoided.

HOMOSEXUALITY

Most Promiscuous

The late Thomas Michael Barrie of San Francisco, California, USA, is documented as having had 23,000 partners. His claim is substantiated by letters, photographs and home movies. The popular Mr Barrie was killed (stabbed) in 1981 by an ex-lover.

Most Unusual Location

The most unusual location for homosexual intercourse to take place is probably the Russian space station MIR. Very little information on this matter is available other than that three cosmonauts were involved in the incident.

The most unusual earthbound location for homosexual intercourse is (allegedly) the centre of the Louisiana Superdome Stadium in front of an audience of over 80,000 people. Further details are not available, while legal proceedings draw to a conclusion.

Highest Altitude

See above.

Lowest Altitude

A notorious and well-documented incident on board a certain American nuclear submarine (consequently dubbed USS *Faggot*) contributed to one of the worst scandals in US naval history. It officially took place at nearly 600 metres below sea level and resulted in 14 able seamen being 'severely disciplined'.

Longest Time

Boris Johannson and Gert Kovak of Stockholm, Sweden, took it in turns on 9 April 1989 to

sodomise each other for a period of 16 hours 27 minutes. The entire event was videotaped.

INCEST

Most Notorious
Count Yuri Vorchev of Romania, who married his mother in 1754, later married their eldest daughter (his sister). They had three sons.

Most Promiscuous
Jerome Krantz of San Diego, USA, was charged in October 1957 with having unlawful sexual intercourse with 16 family members including his mother, five sisters and four brothers. The remaining six persons were his own children. He was further charged with having had unlawful sexual intercourse with three of his nieces, all of whom were under age at the time. Mr Krantz hanged himself in a police cell in March 1958.

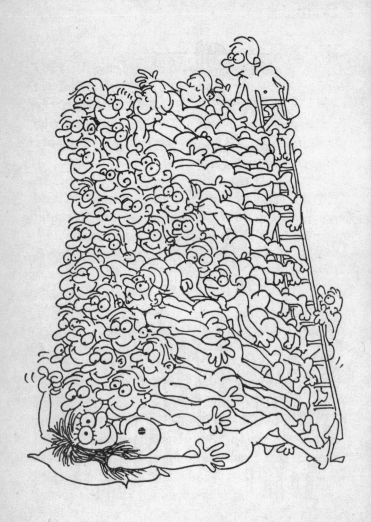

INFIDELITY

Most Promiscuous

Louis Marc Deville of Paris slept with 3567 women after his marriage in 1879. His diary of conquests tallies remarkably well with the observations of his wife, Mirielle Florence, who we must assume therefore was aware of her husband's infidelity.

Mellisa Morgan 'Lovelace' had 3896 extra-marital affairs (verified with postcards and diaries) from 1918 to 1941 when her husband was killed in the war. She did not remarry.

KISS

Longest

Donny Winters and Stella Morenno of Los Angeles, California, USA, kissed throughout July and part of August 1990 (768 hours). Their lips never parted even when they ate, slept and exercised. It has since emerged that their bottom lips were in fact glued together. After careful consideration, it was adjudged that the record should stand.

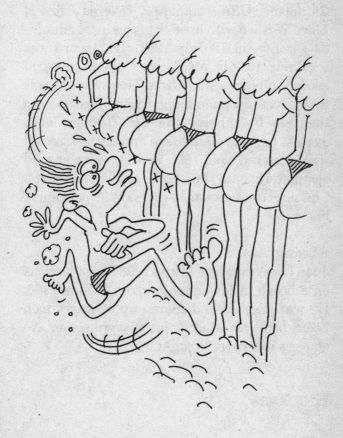

Most Coverage

Maria Antonia Parchez of Los Angeles, California, USA, completely covered 6 ft 4 in Lloyd Warden with lipstick kisses in 24 minutes 34 seconds on 18 July 1991. The record was broken in 1992 by Ms Parchez who knocked 14 seconds off her original time. However, she was later accused of smudging: wiping lipstick onto the skin by rubbing the lips. The evidence against her was plain to see and the new record was declared void. Mr Warden was shaved completely bald for both record attempts. Lipstick coverage was in excess of 99 per cent of his skin.

Kissing 'Ass'

Juan Lopez managed to kiss 1398 ladies' bottoms on a beach in Malaga, Spain, on 7 June 1986. He was grabbed and beaten up by angry men before being arrested 'for his own protection'. No charges were ever brought.

KNICKERS

Largest

The largest pair of knickers ever made had a waist measurement of 110 in. They were

manufactured by Wilson Clarke and Sons Ltd of Rochdale, England, between 1889 and 1902.

Most Flowery
The Warwick Cotton Company of London Ltd produced a pair of knickers in 1952 that had 2478 flowers on them.

Smelliest
The smelliest pair of knickers ever found were probably those discovered in a changing cubicle in a prestigious New York department store in 1990. They were so soiled and unpleasant that a specialist sanitation company had to be called in to remove the offending article and disinfect the entire row of cubicles. The knickers were subsequently incinerated.

MANNEQUIN

Most Obscene
In 1979 a famous New York fashion house and shop arranged 15 window mannequins into an orgy scene in an attempt to attract sale customers. However, the scene was a little too effective and the shop was closed by police after only four hours of trading. The windows were

covered by drapes while the offending dummies were more suitably arranged. 'It was just a bit of harmless fun,' shop manageress Carley Wilkes explained. The shop was fined $1000. Sales, however, soared in the light of all the publicity surrounding the case. New state laws now forbid 'obscene or offensive window displays' and shop managers are deemed liable to personal prosecution if they ignore the stringent guidelines.

Most Offensive

A notorious London punk shop selling 'Nazi-style clothes and accessories' was brought to the attention of the local authorities in 1975. A dummy dressed in said gear was seated on the knee of another mannequin that resembled Her Majesty the Queen. 'He was kissing her and holding a gun up to her head,' the store owner Brett Konieg recalls. Mr Konieg was arrested and his shop closed; however, no charges were ever brought.

New laws now strictly forbid 'offensive' window displays. Any shop that deals in material that could be viewed as offensive must have blacked-out windows and clear warning notices.

Most Erotic

An incredibly lifelike shop mannequin displaying lacy lingerie in a New York department store window in 1988 caused a great deal of fuss. 'She was standing, leaning over a chair, her legs were spread out and she was pouting . . . she stopped the traffic,' recalls a witness. The delicious dummy so entranced male passers-by that one (Eric Lombarde) smashed the window and stole her. 'I had to have her,' Lombarde said. He was fined $600 and ordered to seek professional help.

MASTURBATION

Most Notorious Wanker

Flasher Ricky Forbes of no fixed address was tried and convicted of 16 counts of gross public indecency on 17 September 1962. He was caught in the act in New York's Central Park, 'masturbating in front of a female victim and attempting to throw his semen over her'. Forbes was sent for psychiatric evaluation, declared insane, and institutionalised.

Most Numerous

On 12 September 1987 Clinton Deaves of

Chicago, Illinois, USA, was officially recorded as having masturbated 136 times over a period of 12 hours. He attributed his success to eating oysters and peanut butter sandwiches in large quantities. He only managed to ejaculate five times. The rules state that 'A masturbation will be the attaining of an erection from a flaccid penis by means of the efforts of oneself.'

Clarisse Wilson, late of Richmond, Virginia, USA, was in 1987 one of the first women ever to be medically diagnosed as addicted to masturbation (nymphomasturmania), a condition for which there is no known effective cure. Dr Blake Redwood of Dallas, Texas, USA, when confronted with a similar case prescribed regular daily sexual intercourse as a treatment that he himself administered. He was sentenced to three years' imprisonment in 1989 for gross misconduct.

Preferred Active Alternative
The preferred alternatives to sexual intercourse are: **1** partner's hand relief; **2** oral sex; **3** object relief (feathers, etc.) and **4** a 'hum job', whereby the partner places one or both testicles in his or her mouth and hums the national anthem.

Preferred Inanimate Medium

The preferred inanimate substitutes for the female vagina are: **1** the right hand; **2** the left hand; **3** a grapefruit; **4** a moist (unsliced) brown loaf; **5** balloons (usually three tied together and lubricated, and **6** a plastic male dildo.

The preferred inanimate substitute for the male penis are: **1** the fingers; **2** a banana; **3** plastic dildos and vibrators; **4** baby cucumber and other vegetables; **5** soap and **6** tampon (with applicator).

MUSIC

Most Obscene

'The Rape' (1951), a full orchestral piece by Lucca Perikk of Milan, Italy, is so graphic a score that it has never been performed in public.

Most Offensive

Many people find the national anthem of a particular country deeply offensive. In Great Britain the German national anthem still manages to make the blood of war veterans boil.

Most Erotic

The most erotic piece of music (the piece

preferred by most lovers) is Ravel's 'Boléro'.
(See also **Pop Music**.)

NASAL HAIR

Longest
Claude Michel Faber of Brussels, Belgium, had
nasal hair that was officially recorded as being
on average 5¼ in long. He wore it as a
moustache.

Most Abundant
James Westbridge of Dayton, Ohio, USA, had
such thickly growing nasal hair that he could
not breathe through his nose.

NASAL MUCUS

Longest
The longest dried bogey trail ever officially
verified was found under a table at a certain
well-known public school. It was carefully
measured at 26⅔ in long.

Largest
The largest bogey (snot-knot) ever found was the

size of an acorn and was discovered in a discarded handkerchief in a London department store restaurant in 1989.

Most Horrible

The most horrible deposit of nasal mucus ever verified was probably that of Christopher Ian Lampton of London. On 19 April 1988 he was seen to 'sniff and deposit a large amount of green mucus' on Platform 2 of Euston Underground Station. It was so disgusting that none of the staff would approach it and clear it away. It was eventually dispersed with a fire extinguisher. Lampton was arrested, charged for the offence and later fined £25.

Most Eaten

Eleven-year-old schoolboy Malcolm Stuart Pierce of Bromley, England, was admitted to hospital in 1986 with stomach pains and a nasty cough. He was induced to vomit and produced 'a very large amount of partially dried nasal mucus particles'. It transpired that he had eaten them over a period of three weeks and that they were not all his own. His mother informed the doctor that her son was continually being punished for his 'revolting habit'.

Nasal Mucus Classification Chart

Compiled by Dr Randolph Heart, Consultant Ear, Nose and Throat Specialist, The Abbingdon Clinic, New York City, USA

Type	Size (in)	Shape	Colour
Bogey	¼	round	green
Dabber	¼	oval	green
Comet	¾	streak	light green
Razor	¼	curve	dark green
Splatter	1	spot	light green
Clot Knot	½	round	red/black
Baby Plug	¼	round	green
Dangler	5	thread	green
Ferret	¼	round	green
Pavement Peril	2	spot	green
Hanky Horror	3	spot	red/yellow/green
Cold Clear	3	spread	clear

Marks are given out of 10, 10 being the highest score.

Hardness/ Stickiness		Usual Post- Nasal Location	Mode of Extraction
H2	S9	hanky/sleeve	finger
H3	S8	under table	finger
H2	S9	under bar-stool	finger
H9	S2	on carpet	fingernail
H2	S8	hanky	sneeze
H8	S2	hanky	fingernail
H2	S8	upper lip	snuffle
H2	S9	dangling	sneeze
H7	S4	upper nose	tweezers
H2	S9	pavement	coughflob
H2	S9	hanky/hand	sneeze
H1	S9	tissue	blowout

Stickiest
A 'dabba' found stuck to a London restaurant toilet cubicle door in 1989 could only be removed with a chisel.

Hardest
Joseph Hemlock of Leeds, England, produced 'sizeable snot-knots' that were so hard and sharp that they could cut through a sheet of thick cardboard.

NECROPHILIA

Most Promiscuous
New York undertaker Charles William Rochester admitted in 1867, after being caught in the act, to committing 'unlawful acts' with most of his younger 'female clients'. His intimate diaries seized by the police graphically describe 38 years of unnatural desire. He was sentenced to 15 years with hard labour, but died in prison after serving only three years and five months. He was cremated.

Roger Ian Preston of Kansas City, USA, was officially charged with body-snatching on 7 February 1979. It was alleged that over a period of three years he did unlawfully exhume 16

SLEEPING
BEAUTY
R.I.P

female corpses for the purposes of sexual intercourse. He pleaded insanity and was sent for psychiatric counselling.

Paul Lewis of Vermont, USA, confessed in 1989 to 'digging up' his dead girlfriend, Clara May Bridges, for the purposes of renewing their sexual relationship. It transpired during the hearing that Lewis was besotted with his sweetheart and 'could never love another'. Judge Nathan Parks, on advising psychiatric care, said it was the saddest, most bizarre crime of passion he could ever recall. Ms Bridges was cremated by her family in 1990.

NIPPLES

Largest
Clara Timmamenn of Santa Barbara, California, USA, has nipples that are 2¾ in in diameter and 2¼ in in length when erect.

There are many claims to this title but, as in the case of Candy 'Corky' Kerrigan who boasted nipples the size of 'large champagne corks', it is often later proved that they have been enhanced by cosmetic surgery.

Nipple Classification Chart

Compiled by Dr Janice M. Platt, Senior Consultant Cosmetic Breast Surgery, The Weyer Clinic, Los Angeles, USA

Type	Diameter (in)	Shape	Height (in)
Pinhead	¼	round	fraction
Puppy Nose	1+	oval	N/A
Button	½	round	¼
Grape	¾	grape	½
Bell	¾	bell	½–¾
Doughnut	1	doughnut	¾
Cork	1+	champagne cork	1½+
Bullet	1	bullet	1½+
Superteat	1	finger	2+
Battleship Rivet	2	round	2
Chapel Hatpeg	2	finger	3+
Door Handle	3+	round	3+

Breast Size	Areola	Attraction	Suckling Potential
small	large	small	limited
small/medium	small	fair	limited
small/medium	large	fair	fair
any size	medium	good	good
medium/large	large	good	good
medium/large	small	good	good
large	small	v.good	v.good
large	medium	v.good	v.good
large	medium	excellent	excellent
large	large	excellent	excellent
large	small	v.good	v.good
large	small	good	good

Smallest
There are many cases of women who have no nipples at all. The smallest nipples ever recorded on fully developed breasts belonged to Paula Davi of Portland, Oregon, USA. They measure just ⅛ in in diameter.

Longest
Virginia 'Jugs' Johnston of Los Angeles, California, USA, boasts 4½ in nipples. They have, however, only been officially verified as being 4⅓ in in length and ⅔ in in diameter. It is generally believed that they are natural.

Flattest
Jani Lindqvist of Malmo, Sweden, is one of many unfortunate women who have inverted nipples. Ingrowing nipples can in most cases be corrected by simple surgery.

Most Numerous
It is not uncommon for women and men to have more than two nipples and there are hundreds of cases. Nicky St Clair of Rochester, New York, USA, is well documented as having 16 nipples on her otherwise normal breasts. Only two are functional. David Rees of London had nine nipples on his chest.

Most Pierced
Helena 'Ellen Briggs' Brigstorm of Albuquerque, New Mexico, USA, has 46 rings in each of her nipples, one for each year of her life. (She is 46 not 92.)

ORAL SEX

Most Promiscuous
Freddie 'The Face' Thorn of New York City, USA, had oral sex with 4823 women in one year. He videotaped every one and was shot dead by persons unknown in 1988.

Paul Edward 'Licks Luther' Morton of Atlanta, Georgia, USA, has licked the genitalia of more than 10,000 women over a period of 30 years. (See **Tongue**.)

Most Semen Swallowed
Michelle 'Mony Mony' Monaghan had 1.7 pints of semen pumped out of her stomach in Los Angeles, California, USA, on 16 July 1991.

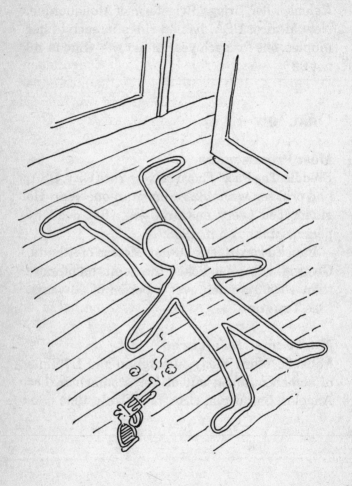

ORGASM

Longest
The longest officially timed female orgasm was enjoyed by Katrina Voss of Copenhagen, Denmark. It was electrically monitored as lasting 23 minutes 14 seconds and was induced and sustained with a vibrator.

Shortest
In medical tests, Juna Karfusst of Gothenburg, Sweden, never managed to sustain an orgasm for more than two seconds.

Most Multiple
Sonja Christianson of Stockholm, Sweden, was officially recorded as having 37 separate vibrator-induced orgasms over a period of an hour.

Most Easily Attained
Mari Volka of Stockholm, Sweden, could reach a self-induced climax in an average time of 3.8 seconds.

Most Difficult to Attain
Many women never experience orgasm. Véronique Mayers of Lyons, France, in exhaus-

Orgasm Classification Chart

Compiled by Drs Ingrid and Hans Vannik, The
Stockholm Institute of Sexual Therapy and
Research, Sweden

Type	Duration (secs)	Stimulation
Dream	30	imagination
Fake	5	obligation
Tickler	8	clitoris
Twitcher	10	clitoris
Bobbler	10	anal sex
Thruster	15	clitoris
Singer	20	intercourse
Smacker	15	intercourse
Humdinger	20	intercourse/clitoris
Cloud 69	30	intercourse/clitoris
Screamer	30	intercourse/clitoris
Raging	30	intercourse
Killer	30	intercourse

Duration times are inclusive of Post Orgasm Muscular
Spasm (POMS). A female orgasm itself rarely exceeds a
few seconds in duration. It is possible, therefore, as in some
cases listed above, for an orgasm to repeat before the end
of the previous orgasmic POMS.

Marks are given out of 10, 10 being the highest score.

Degree of Pleasure	Attainment Time (mins)	Repeat Time (mins)
2	5	2
4	12	2
5	5	8
7	8	8
7	7	8
9	5	4
9	8	10
9	15	15
10	15	15
10	20	20
10	30	5 secs
10+	40	2 secs
10+	40	continuous

tive tests, took an average of 54 minutes to reach a climax.

Most Violent
Gina Violetta de Luise of Tivoli, Italy, had such a violent orgasm during intense sexual intercourse with her lover that she broke his back, killing him instantly. She was indicted for his murder in 1976, but charges were later dropped.

John Stafford of New York City, USA, on reaching orgasm accidentally headbutted his girlfriend 'three or four times'. Ms Evans, who sustained a fractured skull, a broken nose and the loss of four teeth, sued Stafford for grievous bodily harm and was awarded $20,000 in compensation. Stafford still maintains that he remembers nothing of the incident though in an initial statement he claimed that she had butted him.

ORGY

Largest
The largest orgy on record was held in Rome in 68 BC and is documented as having over 10,000 participants.

PAEDOPHILIA

Most Promiscuous
Uri Kassell of the Ukraine has officially been
accredited with sexually assaulting more than
5000 children over a period of 20 years. He was
shot dead by persons unknown in 1961.

PAINTING

Most Obscene
The works of Renaissance artist Camarillo are
generally considered by experts as obscene and
pornographic. 'Camarillo blatantly sacrificed art
for gratuitous titilation, his work and his health
suffered as a result,' Christien de Coet, expert
and collector, told me. 'These pictures are not
erotica they are pornography, very good pornography.'

Most Offensive
There are hundreds of paintings that many people
find offensive for different reasons. It is impossible
to pick out one in particular. A London art dealer
told me, 'The most offensive works in many ways
are modern works that offend the senses and the
intelligence, but make a lot of money.'

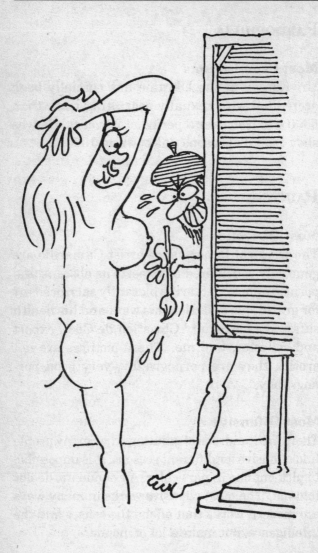

PENIS

Longest
Klaus Bachmann of Munich, Germany, has a penis that is regularly measured at 8¾ in when 'cool' and 14½ in when 'hot'. He is unable to attain a full hard erection or sustain any sort of erection for very long. Competition for this title is intense, but although monstrous claims are numerous, hard medical evidence is not forthcoming.

Shortest
Piers Johansson of Stockholm, Sweden, has a chronically undeveloped penis that is only 1¾ in when erect, the same length as when flaccid. He nonetheless has fathered six children.

Fattest
'Big' Bernardo Scarlatti of Rome, Italy, has a 7¾ in penis that is 3½ in in diameter. 'It is a bigger public attraction than the Leaning Tower of Pisa,' Scarlatti boasts.

Thinnest
Jimi 'The Sting' Santiago of Los Angeles, California, USA, has a 5¾ in penis officially measured as being just ¾ in in diameter. 'I've

had no complaints,' says movie star Jimi.

Most Bent
Rocco Bennelli of Taranto, Italy, has a bent and slightly twisted 6⅛ in penis that has an angle of 87 degrees. A sufferer of Peyronie's Syndrome, the bend is due to fibrous tissues growing on the side of his penis. He has so far resisted the temptation to have the problem surgically corrected.

Most Twisted
Samuel Frederick Tapper of Bolton, England, was medically diagnosed as suffering from Peyronie's Syndrome on 8 September 1991. In this unusual case the fibrous tissues had twisted his penis through nearly 180 degrees, giving it the appearance of being upside down. As a result, the unfortunate Mr Tapper had great difficulty urinating and having sexual intercourse. Corrective surgery in October of the same year has so far proved a great success and a further operation 'should put things back to normal' says surgeon Phillip McIntyre.

Most Powerful
Sammy 'The Crane' Singer of New York City, USA, can lift 114 lb with the base of his erect

4¾ in penis. He hooks the weight onto his penis then lifts it clear of the ground by straightening his legs. 'The tricky part is doing it in front of a crowd. It makes it very difficult for me to get hard enough,' Sammy says. He has developed a special lifting harness for the job after once being nearly castrated when a wire cut through the plastic sheath.

Largest Opening

Mickey 'Studds' has an opening to his penis that can accommodate his entire index finger (¾ x ¾ x 3 in). He uses an inserted fountain pen to sign autographs.

Most Tattooed

Mike 'The Shadow' Loggani has a hundred per cent ink coverage of his body surface including his fully erect penis (right to the top). The procedure, he says, brought tears to his eyes.

Steve Dorsey of Santa Monica, California, USA, has 56 separate tattoos on his penis, many being names.

Most Pierced

Clark Hudson of Los Angeles, California, USA, has 235 rings and 187 studs on his 3 in penis. He was diagnosed as being sexually impotent

Penis Classification Chart

Compiled by Dr Erick Van Lanssing, Senior
Consultant, The Stockholm Institute of Sexual
Therapy and Research, Sweden

Type	Flaccid Length (in)	Diameter (in)	Erection Range (in)
Head	1	1	1–1
Mini	2	1	1–2
Mighty Mini	2	2	2–3
Mr A	3	2	3–5
Fat Larry	4	2½	4–6
Slim Jim	5	1½	5–8
Extra Long	6	2	6–10
Extra Fat	6	2½	6–8
Blenney	2 x 6	2 × 2	6–8 x 2

Female Satisfaction	Time to Achieve Erection	Minutes Sustained	Percentage of Population Affected
poor	3 secs	30+	2
poor	5 secs	30+	3
fair	10 secs	30+	5
good	20 secs	20+	60
v.good	30 secs	15+	10
v.good	45 secs	10+	10
v.good	1 min	5	5
v.v.good	1 min	5	5
v.v.good	2 mins	20 secs	0.2

at the age of 18. 'I thought I might as well do something interesting with it,' he says.

Most Numerous

In 1854 John Scott Thompson of London was recorded as having five perfectly formed penises and three sets of testicles. Surgeons successfully amputated the spare organs in 1856. Since then there have been other similar cases, but details are not publicly available. There are, however, well-documented cases of men having two fully functional penises. Ricardo Perez, Jean Baptisto Dos Santos and William Hunter-Blenney are quite famous for just this reason. Bigenital disorders like these are extremely rare and reliable information is hard to come by.

Legend has it that all the above men were sexual monsters and could use both penises simultaneously. Hunter-Blenney was a certified madman at the age of 21 and Dos Santos had such high amounts of testosterone in his body that he was a 'veritable beast', insatiable in sexual appetite. Sanchez, however, was almost certainly a fraud in that his second penis was not sexually functional, though with his formidable libido he was able to fool many of his women friends into thinking that he used both. In all three cases it remains impossible to

separate the facts from the folklore and thus doubts remain.

Most Unusual Location

In a very rare medical condition known as Shelley's Disorder the male penis, and in most cases the testicles as well, do not develop in the correct place. John David Bruce of London was, in 1789, the first case on medical record. His penis was situated just below his navel. Pancho 'Frankie' Bollo of Uruguay is the most recent celebrated case, with penis and testicles growing out of his right thigh. The organs are non-functional and would have been removed years ago if they hadn't brought fame and fortune to the family involved.

Longest Foreskin

Kelvin Hughes of Devon, England, is well documented as having a rare disorder that has led to him having a foreskin that is 6¾ in longer than his penis. Circumcision is at this time being seriously considered.

PHLEGM

See **Bile and Phlegm**.

PHOTOGRAPH

Most Obscene
Robert Sackville's photographs of naked men in various stages of heterosexual, homosexual and sadomasochistic arousal are rarely exhibited for long, such is the outcry from a respectable public. Sackville revels in this notoriety which is, in his own words, good for business.

Most Offensive
Ellery Kline's staged photographs of people (nuns, priests, rabbis, etc.) doing things they shouldn't are deliberately designed to shock and offend. Images featuring racism, blasphemy (anti-Catholicism in particular) and anti-Semitism (unusual as Kline is himself Jewish) are his speciality. 'As long as people buy my work, I'll keep taking pictures,' he says.

POP MUSIC

Most Obscene
There are many claims for this dubious honour but 'Relax' by Frankie Goes To Hollywood and 'Animal (Fuck Like a Beast)' by the rock group WASP (White Anglo-Saxon Protestant) are top

contenders. Both songs were extremely popular and reached the number one spot in their specific charts.

Most Offensive
'Friggin' in the Riggin' (On The Good Ship Venus)' by The Sex Pistols managed to offend just about everybody (as did most of their songs) when it was first released.

Video
The most offensive and obscene pop video was 'Cuming at You' by the Dickheads, released in 1991. The video features five erect (except the drummer) penises dressed up as musicians that wobbled and wilted their way through the song. They were refused a spot on *Top of the Pops* as 'they were blatantly miming'.

Most Erotic
The pop song preferred by 'lovers' is 'Unchained Melody', first performed by the Righteous Brothers. It is closely followed by 'I Will Always Love You', written and sung by Dolly Parton, and '(Everything I Do) I Do It For You', performed by Bryan Adams.

POSTCARD

Naughtiest
There are millions of naughty postcards sent through the post each year and thousands to choose from. It is impossible to say which is the naughtiest.

Most Popular
The most popular naughty postcards in England are the seaside cartoon cards which have been around for many years. In second place are postcards showing Page 3 models in topless poses. In America, postcards depicting raunchy California girls are extremely popular and are also sold in shops all over the world.

PROSTITUTE

Highest Paid
Serina Hartford of Los Angeles, California, USA, was reputed to have earned more than $50,000 a night according to the United States Revenue Department in 1984. 'Are you just a hooker?' she was asked shortly after her arrest. 'A damn good one,' she replied. Ms Hartford was caught through accepting payment by stolen credit cards.

Mimi Solomam of New York City, USA, earned $13.6 million over a period of ten years. She was jailed for three years for tax evasion in 1989. 'Just my luck to get a judge I never slept with,' she stated, referring to Judge Mary Winnock.

Hardest Working
Lola Bevin of New York City, USA, averaged 46 clients a night in 1991 according to her seized accounts books. 'People think it's an easy job,' she told the court. 'They should try it.'

PUBERTY

Earliest
Gina Coleman of Baltimore, Maryland, USA, reached puberty (began menstruating) at 6 years 5 months and 23 days old.

Bobby Slinger of Charleston, West Virginia, USA, was medically diagnosed as being pubescent at 7 years 11 months and 13 days old.

Latest
Caroline Catherine Jordan of Philadelphia, New Jersey, USA, did not start menstruating until she was 46 years 4 months and 17 days old. She is quoted as saying 'It wasn't worth the wait.'

Michael Bergdorf of New York City, USA, did not become sexually active until he was 38 years 10 months and 18 days old. He is quoted as saying 'It was worth the wait.'

PUBIC HAIR

Longest
Maoni Vi of Cape Town, South Africa, has hair measuring 32 in from the armpits and 28 in from the groin.

Most Prolific
Corrine Verity Fennitton's pubic hair was so thick and bushy that she was unable to have sexual intercourse with her husband. She apparently never shaved it off and their marriage remained unconsummated.

QUESTION

Rudest
The rudest questions ever asked on a chat show are:
1 *Oprah* 'I'd like to ask you [Oprah] how can you look at yourself on TV, you're so gross?'

2 *Dame Edna* 'So, are you menstruating at the moment possum?'

3 *Donoghue* 'Phil, do you really enjoy jerking people off?'

4 *Question Time* 'Does the panel think that Sir Robin is an arsehole?'

RADIO

Most Offensive
Germany Calling and *Tokyo Rose* are two good examples of wartime propaganda radio broadcasts that offended everyone who was meant to be listening.

Most Obscene
There are a number of pirate radio stations offering sexually explicit shows, particularly in America. They are banned by law, of course, and have to move around to avoid being caught.

A notorious play broadcast on a famous English radio station rocked the nation in 1961 with its obscene audiosexual content. It was taken off the air after only two episodes and was never heard of again. 'We tried to re-edit it of course but it just didn't work,' the producer explained. 'Nowadays it would be considered pretty tame, but radio in this country still has very strong undercurrents of respectability. You can see explicit sex on BBC 1, but you can't hear it on Radio 4.'

SADOMASOCHISM

Most Depraved
Obtaining sexual gratification by inflicting or receiving pain was understood long before the Marquis de Sade (who lends his name to the practice of sadism) set down literary guidelines. It is still, however, considered to be dangerous and perverted (which is why it is so popular). All acts of sadomasochism are most depraved and it is impossible to grade them in any way. (See **Books**.)

SALIVA

Greatest Distance Attained
At the annual indoor 'Flobbing Festival Finals' held in a well-known American college, Don 'Gumball' Warner propelled a 'Gob of Flob' an incredible 38 ft. The rules are strict: competitions are always held indoors to prevent wind

assistance, and three judges are always on hand to ensure that there is no foul play. David Rameres in a similar competition was barred for a year after being caught using a 'booster'. This was a small ice cube that carried the saliva a great distance before it dropped off and was marked. The ice is very difficult to detect and is supposed to melt before the 'flob' is cleared away. But it wasn't on this occasion. As well as a 12-month ban, Rameres was sentenced by a disciplinary board to be 'Gozzed' (spat on by his fellow competitors for one minute).

Greatest Amount Produced

Larry 'Hubba' Tennison of Columbia, South Carolina, USA, salivated to an extraordinary degree. He could not speak for fear of drooling terribly down his shirt. Overactive saliva glands are quite common, but Mr Tennison's case is by far the worst. Drug treatment does not apparently help much, as it just dries up the mouth, creating an even worse problem.

SEMEN

Most Produced

Henrik Baur of Bonn, Germany, produced on 12

September 1991 0.14 of a pint of semen from a single ejaculation. This is enough to fill a shot glass.

Most Potent

The highest sperm count on medical record was produced by Carlo Gianaldi. Precise details cannot be published on legal grounds, but I can say that it was many times greater than the average. It may be of interest to note that over 500 million sperm are usually present in the semen of a single ejaculation.

Oldest

The 'Ice Man' of the Alps, who is believed to be 5000 years old, was discovered with his testicles still intact. He had been frozen so quickly that the sperm they contained was in cryogenic suspension. It is believed possible to thaw out the seminal fluid and use it to fertilise a human egg. Female volunteers willing to be fertilised by the ancient sperm are apparently large in number.

Seminal Fluid Range Chart

Compiled by Professor Ian Bradley, Head of
Physics, Gladstone University, Montreal, Canada.
Author of *The Aerodynamics Of Fluids* (1984)

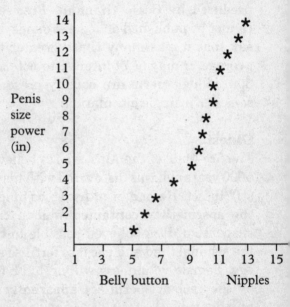

Average range is shown on the left of the chart, range limit
on the right. A long penis does not necessarily mean that
semen will be projected further on ejaculation than a short
penis. Indeed, in a long 'barrel' the force of friction acts
upon the fluid, effectively slowing it down. However, the
first law of hydraulics (a liquid cannot be compressed)
ensures that the semen maintains its initial velocity to
some degree. Thus, seminal fluid is surprisingly consistent

142

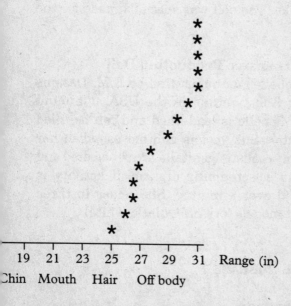

| 19 | 21 | 23 | 25 | 27 | 29 | 31 | Range (in) |

Chin   Mouth   Hair   Off body

in its average range. These facts are also applicable to
ranges inside the confines of the vagina: penetration and
performance (fertilisationally speaking) only show a
marked difference when there is a huge variation in penis
size.

The performance of any single penis is not at all
consistent. The above chart, therefore, should be treated
as an approximate guide only.

Sex Doll

Most Lifelike
A rubber doll made for the British film *Wilt* was so lifelike that the producers were inundated with calls from people wishing to purchase 'her' or the like. The doll was specially made for the film.

Most Expensive Production Doll
'Hot Michelle', manufactured by E.M. Designs of Hong Kong, retails in the USA at around $2000. Michelle is lead-lined and can be filled with water. She 'moans and moves' when her 'incredibly realistic' genitalia are penetrated and even has a 'screaming orgasm' if activity is continued over a minute. She comes in three different models (oriental, black, white).

Sexual Disease

Most Common
The most common sexually transmitted disorder is the crab louse. The most common disease is herpes.

Most Dangerous
The most life-threatening sexually transmitted disease is HIV which can lead to AIDS. (Wear a condom.)

Most Unpleasant
The most unpleasant curable sexually transmitted disease is syphilis closely followed by gonorrhoea.

SEXUAL INTERCOURSE

Longest Time
Alain Simminon and Renee Clouse of San Diego, California, USA, made love continuously for 86.8 hours in May 1978. The event was filmed and as such is one of the longest pornographic films on record.

Most Pleasurable
When Michael Deirks and Rita Sampson made love in Room 207 of a famous New York hotel, no less than 187 people complained about the noise. The management was forced to intervene and on entering the room found it completely wrecked and the lovers still entwined and screaming on the ruffled carpet.

146

Highest Altitude
The highest altitude officially recorded for sexual intercourse was that attained during a Soviet experiment involving a male and female cosmonaut. Its purpose was to ascertain whether or not conception in a weightless environment was possible. The experiment was carried out on the MIR space station. No further details are available, though it is widely believed to be part of a Soviet plan to have the first child conceived and born in space by the year 2000.

Lowest Altitude
There are numerous reports on file of persons claiming to have had heterosexual intercourse while submerged in a submarine. None of these claims can be verified.

Most Unusual Location
Glyn Western and Veronica Lang of Los Angeles, California, USA, were spotted making love on top of a speeding train. When they had finished they climbed down and were arrested. No charges were ever brought.

Harry Macks and Jo Preston of Dallas, Texas, USA, in a celebrated stunt, made love wired to the wing of an aeroplane which flew upside down. 'It was an exhilarating experience,' said

Macks after the event. Preston commented 'The hardest part was putting the condom on, but we had to use one, that was the whole point of the show.' The stunt, suitably censored, was later used in a safe-sex campaign.

Highest Speed/Rate of Penetration
Thomas Vell of Oslo, Norway, performed at 252 strokes a minute (4.2 per second) in Stockholm in 1991. 'Good technique and suitable lubrication are essential,' Vell explains.

Most Positions
Ulrich Rekka and Lotte Verne performed in 467 different positions in an hour (a new position every eight seconds). Complete penetration twice is required for the position to be affirmed. 'The penis need not be withdrawn in order to attain a new position', which I am reliably informed can save 'vital seconds, particularly when clocking'.

Dr Sultan Ghani said in 1976, 'There are over 500 recognised sexual positions, but many of these are just clocks, that is to say, a minor variant (12 in all) of a single position.' This means that a man can lie on a woman in a position of 12 o'clock through to 11 o'clock.

Oldest Loving Couple
Duane Allan Lavender of Fort Lauderdale, Florida, USA, and his wife Marcia still regularly enjoy sexual intercourse twice a week in spite of the fact that they are 87 and 76 years old respectively.

Youngest Loving Couple
In Milan, Italy, in 1974 it was widely reported that a boy (12) and his girlfriend (7) were caught having sexual intercourse in a Fiat by the girl's mother.

SODOMY

Most Promiscuous Sodomite
Norman Henry Rossett of Norwich, England, catalogued in great detail no less than 26,457 accounts of buggery (all with different persons of both sexes) between the years 1642 and 1687. His diary lists the particulars of large parties at which he would bugger up to 40 people at one time, 'but releasing [ejaculating] only several times'.

STAGE ACT

Most Offensive
Kerry Hunt and her 7 ft reticulated python Fred performed regularly at venues throughout the USA in the 1970s. After an erotic dance, Ms Hunt would allow Fred to enter her vagina. The act and many others were banned after animal rights protesters petitioned Congress.

Most Obscene
Mary Louise 'Maria Mink' Carter smoked a cigarette with her vagina while on stage and sang 'See what the boys in the back room will have'. She retired in 1984 with cervical cancer thought to have been caused by her unusual talent; this, however, has not been conclusively proved.

TELEVISION

Most Obscene
There are a great number of satellite and cable television stations that cater for all tastes in obscene material. New government guide-lines in Great Britain may soon outlaw programmes such as *Red Hot Dutch*, a sex

show that is particularly popular.

Most Offensive
Many television programmes are broadcast each year which offend unsuspecting viewers, be it by foul language, sex, nudity, racial slurs, dead bodies or cruelty to animals or, in some cases, all of these.

TESTICLES

Largest
Rodderick Hanson of Richmond, Virginia, USA, has unusually swollen testicles that measure 4¼ in (left) and 3⅛ in (right) in diameter. Despite their size, production is average. The cause of the swelling is not known for certain, but the unfortunate Mr Hanson did contract mumps at the age of 18. The painful experience may well have left its mark.

Smallest
Mark Thomas Reese of Atlanta, Georgia, USA, has testicles that measure only ⅔ in. They are, however, reasonably functional and Mr Reese has fathered two daughters.

Most Yielding
See **Semen**.

Greatest Number
Richard George Stansford of London was
medically diagnosed in 1967 as having five fully
formed testicles in a single scrotum, all of which
were 'plumbed in'. It is not uncommon for a man
to have more than a pair; there are hundreds of
cases. Simple surgery can put the matter right,
indeed, testicles can now be transplanted and
there is a great demand for them. Mr Stansford's
biggest problem was the huge amounts of
testosterone in his body (up to three times the
average), and he was a 'giant sexual athlete'.

Most Unfortunate
There are many cases on record of men whose
scrotum and testicles have grown above their
penis (upside down). They are nonetheless quite
functional. Far less common is the growth of
testicles in other parts of the body. (See **Penis**.)

TONGUE

Longest
The longest human tongue ever recorded was

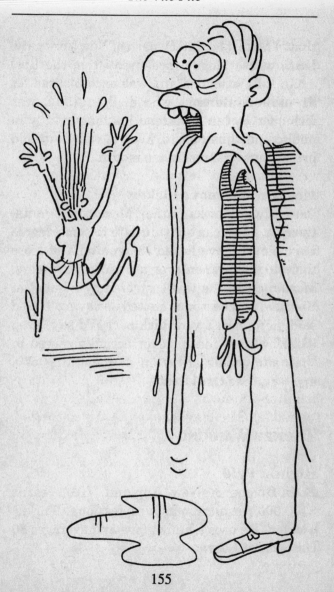

155

that of Matt 'The Cat' Henson of New York City, USA, whose tongue measured (from the lips) 4¾ in fully extended and was once insured for $1 million. Henson, who died in 1984, was forbidden by law to extend his tongue fully in public and thus had to 'keep it rolled up and pressed into the roof of his mouth'.

Most Promiscuous Licker
Paul Edward 'Licks Luther' Morton of Atlanta, Georgia, USA, can substantiate to some degree his claim to have licked the genitalia of more than 10,000 women over a period of 30 years. Morton claims he was castrated by a bullet in Vietnam and was once quoted as saying 'If God said, here, here's your dick back, I'd say "keep it".' However, 'Licks' never actually served in Vietnam, so his affliction is something of a mystery. (See **Oral Sex**.)

TURKEY WANKING

Highest Paid
Ross Givens of New England, USA, earns $100,000 per annum as a professional 'Turkey Tickler'. He uses a mink glove and averages 30 turkeys per hour.

TURKEYS

Most Efficient

Michael Duncun Higgins of Clinton, Oklahoma, USA, 'wanked' 92 turkeys in one hour on 6 November 1989. He claims he can do over a hundred in the time, but this has not been verified.

Despite the jokes, turkey wanking is a serious business. A relieved male turkey will not chase female turkeys and neither therefore will lose any weight.

URINATION

Greatest Distance

Peter James Clark of Springfield, Illinois, USA, projected a jet of urine 21 ft 7 in on 7 January 1991. He retired from public performances in 1992 after severely rupturing his bladder with his incredibly strong urinary muscles.

Greatest Altitude

Peter James Clark of Springfield, Illinois, USA, attained an altitude of 15 ft 3 in with a jet of urine on 7 January 1991.

Longest Time

David Ian Lyons of Glasgow, Scotland, urinated

159

constantly for 24 minutes 46 seconds on 14 May
1984, and has come very close to repeating the
feat on several occasions. Preparation involves
the consumption of ten pints of strong cider, the
last three being 'supped whilst pissing'.

Greatest Amount Swallowed
Jurgen Prokov from Hannover, Germany, drank
nine pints of his own urine when he was lost in
the Pacific Ocean for 16 days in 1975. 'It kept
me alive' he told reporters when he had
recovered from his ordeal.

Longest Time Waited
The longest time anyone has voluntarily
abstained from urination is 47 hours 34 minutes
by Aubrey Castle of Plymouth, England. In a
later repeat of his record attempt he suffered a
ruptured bladder and was forced to retire.

VAGINA

Longest
Shani Stanton of St Paul, Minnesota, USA, has
a relaxed vaginal opening measured at 4⅓ in.

Vagina Classification Chart

Compiled by Dr Michelle Rocquefort, Consultant
Gynaecologist, The Rocquefort Clinic, Santa
Monica, California, USA

Type	Size (in)	Initial Grip	Attraction
Tight Fit	1	great	5
Juicy Lucy	2	v.good	10
Room For Manoeuvre	3	good	8
Baby Boom	4	fair	7
Lost In Space	5	poor	6
Black Hole	6	v.poor	5
Cavern Club	7	none	3

Marks are given out of 10, 10 being the highest score.

Sensuality	Risk of Flatulence	Arousal Time (secs)
great	great	10
great	great	20
good	great	30
good	fair	30
fair	little	45
poor	none	60
v.poor	none	60+

Smallest
Ella Carpenter of Toronto, Canada, had at the age of 26 a vaginal opening that measured only ⅔ in. Reconstruction surgery in 1987 successfully corrected the matter.

Most Cavernous
Linda Manning of Los Angeles, California, USA, could without preparation completely insert a lubricated football (American) into her vagina. Although the female vagina is incredibly elastic and can cope with the passing through of a sizeable baby, to place a large object back inside is, I am reliably informed, extremely difficult. The extraordinary Ms Manning died in an automobile accident in 1989.

Tightest
The greatest recorded force applied by vaginal muscles is 22 psi (enough to crush a ripe apple) exerted by Carmine Brooks of Seattle, Washington, USA, in 1986. She was banned by law from performing this feat in public and retired in 1988 having reputably earned in excess of $1 million.

Most Tattooed
Tess Evans of New York City, USA, has 98 per

cent coverage of her vulva. The tattoo is in the form of a black triangle of pubic hair, of which she has none.

Rachelle Marissio of Los Angeles, California, USA, has five internal vaginal tattoos: a rose, a snake, the Stars and Stripes, a submarine and the word 'heaven'.

VARICOSE VEINS

Most Horrible
Lilly Ann Marsh of Stockport, England, had 'probably the worst varicose veins on medical record'. The veins in question stood 'very proud of the skin, and appeared to be knotted, bulgy and discoloured'. Ms Marsh obtained expensive corrective surgery on the National Health, and is now quite happy. 'People don't understand how awful it is to have bad legs,' she says, blaming her condition on 'having to bear five children'.

VEGETABLE

Most Suggestive
Careful examination of a large carrot grown by Frank Hodgkinson of Southampton, England,

showed that it had not been tampered with in any way and did indeed resemble a 'very good' penis. It later transpired that the carrot had been grown inside a metal moulding. The technique has now been improved and Mr Hodgkinson makes a great deal of money from his unusual vegetables.

VOMIT

Greatest Distance Attained
The greatest distance ever attained by an expelled jet of vomit is 16 ft 5 in by Lloyd Cornish of Pittsburgh, Pennsylvania, USA. He accredits the feat to eating a 'bad tuna fish and salami pizza a few hours before'.

Greatest Altitude Attained
The greatest altitude attained for expelled vomit is 12 ft 9 in by Ian Mark Bannerman of Denver, Colorado, USA. The event took place in a private hospital and vomit had to be cleaned off the ceiling (hence the accuracy of the measurement).

Greatest Amount
David George Webster-Evans of London did, on 19 February 1986, produce 18 lb 9 oz of vomit

in a taxi cab on the Strand in London. He was
fined £20 for the cost of cleaning up the mess.

Most Horrible
In 1987 a large and lengthy deposit of 'vile
smelling' vomit on the pavement outside a well-
known department store in London prevented a
substantial number of customers from entering
the premises. It was three hours before the mess
was cleared up, by which time the store was
practically deserted.

Most Unfortunate
During a prestigious American pool competition
in front of nearly a thousand paying spectators,
a well-known player 'puked his guts all over the
table'. The match was abandoned.

WARTS

Greatest Number
Harry Gibbons of Glasgow, Scotland, had 176
warts on his body in 1988. A large majority were
on his hands and face and had to be treated with
lasers. The cause of such a great infestation is
unknown.

Most Unfortunate

Walter Goffie is one of many men who have genital warts; however, the unfortunate Mr Goffie of Hereford, England, has over 200 on his penis which is very rare. Again, laser treatment has been applied and they should all be gone by the end of 1994.

WORDS

Most Offensive

The most offensive word in the English language is generally considered to be 'cunt', a vulgar reference to female genitalia or a stupid or unpleasant person. The second most offensive word is 'twat', which has an almost identical meaning to the word 'cunt', but which in addition is often used to describe the punching or striking of a person deemed to be, in the eyes of the assailant, the said 'cunt'.

The third most offensive word is 'muthafucker'. This can also be described as a phrase and split into two words 'mutha fucker' and can be further extended to 'sick mutha fucker'. In all forms it serves as a reference to someone who has regular sexual intercourse with their natural mother or in some cases to someone who has sexual intercourse with a pregnant woman.

The most offensive phrase is 'cock sucker'. This may be directed at either a male or a female who it is suggested regularly sucks a male penis.

Most Used

The most frequently used offensive word in the English language is 'shit' (also 'shite'). This is a vulgar reference to faeces both human or animal or anything deemed to be unpleasant or less than satisfactory.

The second most often used offensive word is 'fuck', relating to sexual intercourse, also used in the phrases 'fuck it', to have sexual intercourse with; 'fuck off', go away and have sexual intercourse; and 'fucked', suffering from an excess of sexual intercourse or generally dysfunctional, tired or dead.

In equal third place are 'tit', meaning a woman's breast or a stupid person, and 'wanker' a person prone to excessive masturbation.

X-RATED

Most X-rated

The most X-rated film/video is *The Exorcist 2*. On an official distributor's poster it was billed as being XXXXXXXXXXXXXXXXXX (18) rated.

Y-FRONTS

Largest
The largest pair of Y-fronts ever made was manufactured by Wilson Clarke Ltd of Rochdale, England, and had a waist measurement of 110 in.

Smelliest
The smelliest pair of Y-fronts on record was discovered in a telephone kiosk in Brighton, England, in 1985. The 'badly soiled underpants' gave off such a stench that the phonebox was not used for 78 days.

Most Skidmarked
The most skidmarked Y-fronts ever to be put on public display belonged to 'The Phantom Arse Rubber' of Oxford, England. With 56 officially verified lines of faecal deposits the Phantom's underpants were the unanimous winners of an unusual university competition.

ZIT

Largest
The largest zit or acne spot ever mentioned on medical record belonged to Duane Lester Williams of Chicago, Illinois, USA. It measured 'just under an inch in diameter'.

Most Horrible
Peter Steven Mendham of Lincoln, England, was so badly covered in weeping spots that he was suspended from his school for five weeks. His very appearance caused staff and pupils alike to be 'quite sick'. The unfortunate boy's parents were forced to take legal action against the school and their son was eventually reinstated. As in most cases, his skin complaint soon cleared up.

Popping
On 9 July 1987 Carl Stuart Chadwick of Rugby, England, 'popped' (squeezed) a zit and projected a detectable amount of yellow pus a distance of 7 ft 1 in. In the same competition, Paul Samuel Baker-Harrison 'popped' 34 zits in the space of one minute.

   Although there have since been many claims on both these records, none have been verified to the satisfaction of the IFZPs (International Federation of Zit Poppers).

More Non-fiction from Headline:

THE UFO ENCYCLOPEDIA

THE MOST COMPREHENSIVE BOOK ON UFOLOGY EVER WRITTEN

COMPILED AND EDITED BY

JOHN SPENCER

FOR THE BRITISH UFO RESEARCH ASSOCIATION

Compiled by one of the world's leading authorities
on the subject, THE UFO ENCYCLOPEDIA is an
authoritative, level-headed and witty reference book
covering all aspects of the UFO phenomenon.
It includes:

* Over 1,000 entries and over 70 colour and black
and white photos

* In-depth analyses of celebrated cases including the
Gulf Breeze Sightings, the Pascagoula Abduction
and the Trindade Island photographs

* First-hand accounts of alien abductions

* Rare photographs and previously unknown cases

* The latest information on related phenomena
including corn circles and the Bermuda Triangle

THE UFO ENCYCLOPEDIA

- a comprehensive manual for professionals and
amateurs alike.

NON-FICTION/REFERENCE   0 7472 3494 9

A selection of non-fiction from Headline